SURVIVING THE MEGATSUNAMI

BookLife
PUBLISHING

©2023
BookLife Publishing Ltd.
King's Lynn, Norfolk
PE30 4LS, UK

A catalogue record for this
book is available from the
British Library.

ISBN: 978-1-80505-022-3

Written by:
Madeline Tyler
Adapted by:
Sam Thompson
Edited by:
Kirsty Holmes
Designed by:
Jasmine Pointer

FSC
www.fsc.org
MIX
Paper from
responsible sources
FSC® C113515

AN INTRODUCTION TO BOOKLIFE RAPID READERS...

Packed full of gripping topics and twisted tales, BookLife Rapid Readers are perfect
for older children looking to propel their reading up to top speed. With three levels
based on our planet's fastest animals, children will be able to find the perfect point
from which to accelerate their reading journey. From the spooky to the silly, these
roaring reads will turn every child at every reading level into a prolific page-turner!

CHEETAH

The fastest animals on land, cheetahs will be taking
their first strides as they race to top speed.

MARLIN

The fastest animals under water, marlins will be blasting through
their journey.

FALCON

The fastest animals in the air, falcons will be flying at top speed as they tear
through the skies.

Photo Credits – Images are courtesy of Shutterstock.com. With thanks to Getty Images, Thinkstock Photo and iStockphoto.
Recurring images – mycteria, benchart, Andrii_Malysh, Bohdan Populov, Anastasiia Veretennikova, Francois Poirier,
MaryDesy, vladimir3d. Cover – Zerbor, jakkapan, nayuki minase. 4–5 – Andrey Yurlov, Krakenimages.com, Bignai. 6–7 –
Ryan Janssens, Semnic. 8–9 – Gareth_Bargate, Michael O'Keene, Jeka. 10–11 – tunasalmon. 12–13 – Narongsak Nagadhana,
lynx_v, Andrew VP. 14–15 – Simon Annable, Wang LiQiang. 16–17 –Anatoliy Karlyuk, Alex Izeman, Bruno Passigatti, Mike_shots,
me_slavka. 18–19 – Chatham172, kasakphoto. 20–21 – Ronnie Chua, Mark Rademaker, Ivan Kurmyshov. 22–23 – austinding,
Phonix_a Pk.sarote. 24–25 –john paul slinger, Fly_and_Dive. 26–27 – Ryan Janssens, Semnic. 28–29 – mimagephotography,
Youkonton. 30–31 – PrimeMockup.

CONTENTS

PAGE 4   A Wall of Water

PAGE 8   Supersized Tsunami

PAGE 12   Stop, Look, Listen

PAGE 16   Tools to Survive

PAGE 20   Advice? Run!

PAGE 24   Your Next Steps

PAGE 26   The Fallout

PAGE 30   Recap: The Disaster Checklist

PAGE 31   Glossary

PAGE 32   Index

Words that look like this are explained in the glossary on page 31.

A WALL OF WATER

Have you ever been in the sea? Did you swim? Maybe you went surfing. But then…

HOW TO READ TSUNAMI:

tsu	na	mi
SOO	NAH	MEE

The ground rumbles. You hear the rush of water. You turn to see a wall of water in the distance.

IT'S A MEGATSUNAMI…

You are about to become a survival expert. You will need to if you are going to make it through the megatsunami alive.

This handbook will tell you everything you need to know. Keep it close.

A tsunami is a set of giant waves. They can be 30 metres high!

The waves travel at 1,000 kilometres per hour. They can be five minutes apart. That means it is hard to know when the tsunami is over.

The Earth has four layers. The crust is the outermost layer. It is made up of large slabs of rock called plates.

The plates sometimes grind and jolt against each other. This can cause earthquakes. An earthquake pushes ocean water up until... TSUNAMI!

TSUNAMI

Think a tsunami sounds bad? Imagine staring into the heart of a megatsunami! These waves are almost twice the height of a normal tsunami.

The wave would be taller than most buildings. Your school would become a swimming pool.

How would a megatsunami be caused? If a lot of land slid down a mountain or cliff into the sea, it would push the water up.

A large <u>meteorite</u> falling from the sky would do the same. A huge wall of water would be formed.

Danger zones are places where tsunamis are likely to happen. The Ring of Fire is a danger zone in the Pacific Ocean.

The Ring of Fire is on the edge of one of Earth's plates. Nine out of ten earthquakes happen here.

RING OF FIRE

The largest ever recorded megatsunami happened in Alaska, US, in 1958. An earthquake caused a <u>landslide</u>.

It made waves over 500 metres tall. Luckily, megatsunamis like this are very rare.

STOP. LOOK. LISTEN

So, you have seen the signs. A megatsunami may be on the way. How can you be sure?

One of the first signs is an earthquake or landslide. Can you hear a loud rumble? Is the ground shaking? Be alert!

Keep an eye out for warnings on TV, online or on the radio. Scientists who <u>detect</u> a tsunami will use these things to warn you.

Scientists are trained to notice odd patterns in the ocean. Make sure to listen for their warnings.

Are you near the sea? You can tell if a megatsunami might start by looking at the water.

Is the water moving back quickly, away from the land? If it is, that is a sure sign a giant wave is coming.

Do you think you are smarter than a flamingo?

Well, they have been known to flee a tsunami before humans even know what is going on!

Check your pets and other animals. Are they acting strangely? It might be a sign.

TOOLS TO SURVIVE

So, there is definitely a megatsunami coming. Have you got a mega survival kit to tackle it? What do you mean, 'no'?

You will need a radio to stay up to date. You will need batteries, too. All the power will soon be off.

When the electricity is gone, you will need light. Make sure to pack a strong torch and even more batteries.

Escaping a tsunami is dangerous. You will need a first aid kit. It needs to have plasters, bandages and medicines in it.

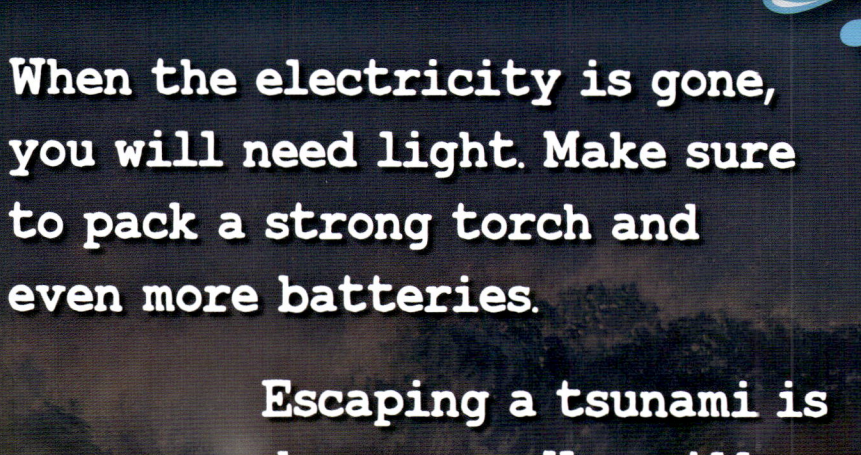

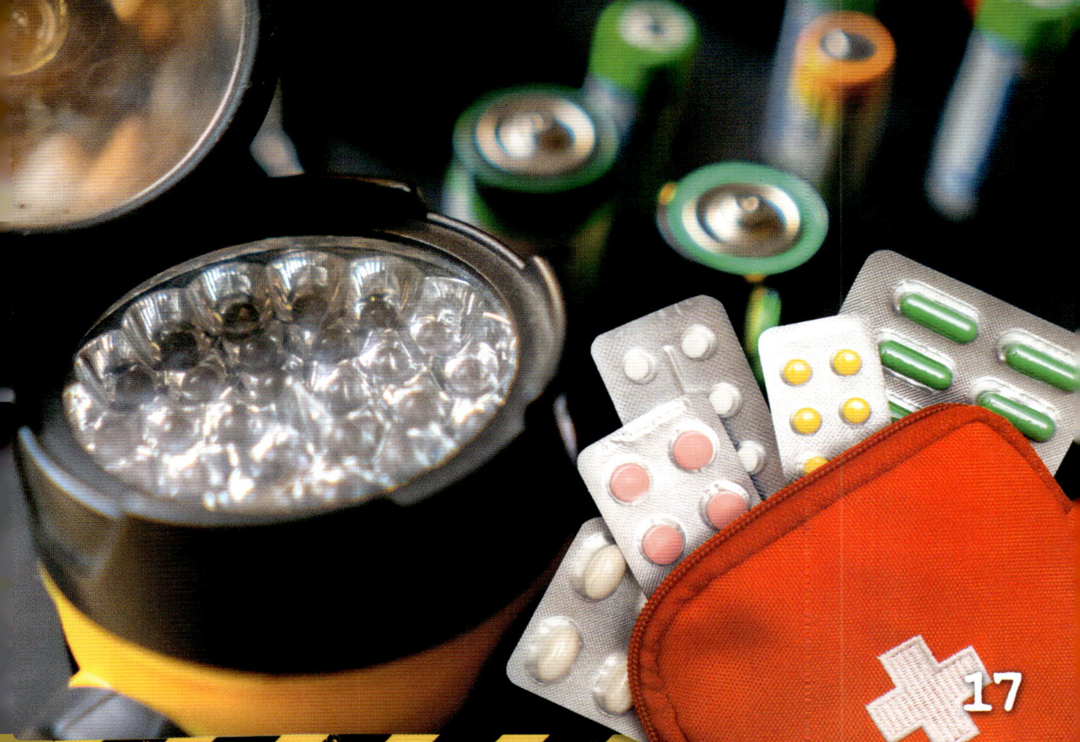

It will not be long before the hunger strikes. You need to get lots of food in cans quickly. Oh, and a can opener, of course!

You can get all sorts of food in cans. You might find beans, soup, custard or even cake!

Do not forget, there might be lots of water around, but it will be salty. Humans should not drink salty water.

Even fresh water in rivers and lakes could be dirty and make you ill. You will need lots of bottled water to stay healthy.

ADVICE?

RUN!

Are you prepared? Good. How fast can you run?

Grab your megatsunami mega survival kit and tell your family to follow you! Just hope your home stays safe while you are gone.

Do not hang around to take a selfie with the waves. Get away from the coast and head inland.

Is there a car around? Get in and drive quickly. You will need to be faster than the giant wave.

21

Are you still there? Well done for surviving so far! If there has been an earthquake, watch out for broken roads.

Try to stick to large, open spaces. The last thing you want is a building falling over in your path.

It is time to start heading up. You need to be high up if you are to stay truly safe.

Aim to be around 30 metres higher than sea level. Keep climbing as high as you can. Then, get ready for a very long wait.

YOUR NEXT STEPS

You should be able to see everything happening from high up. Wait here until the tsunami is over. Stay put!

Aftershocks might happen. They could create more tsunamis. Listen to your radio for news that it is safe to return.

Stay alert if you are going back to a city or town. Buildings might be weak now because of the waves.

An aftershock could bring a building down at any minute. Is that building shaking? Move away from it, quickly.

THE FALLOUT

Most of the transport links around you will be damaged. It will be hard for people to move around.

That means food deliveries might be rare. Thank goodness you have your survival kit!

Even after the megatsunami has stopped, your house might still be under water.

That does not make it a swimming pool. That makes it dangerous. Try to find a shelter to stay in with other survivors.

You might need to <u>ration</u> your bottled water. The left-over water will probably have dirty rubbish and waste in it.

It may be quite some time before the sea water drains away. It is important to help others until this happens.

The clean-up after a megatsunami could take years. Right now, you should be pleased you made it this far.

You faced the force of a megatsunami. Keep strong. You can survive the aftermath, too.

RECAP: THE DISASTER

CHECKLIST

How to survive the megatsunami:

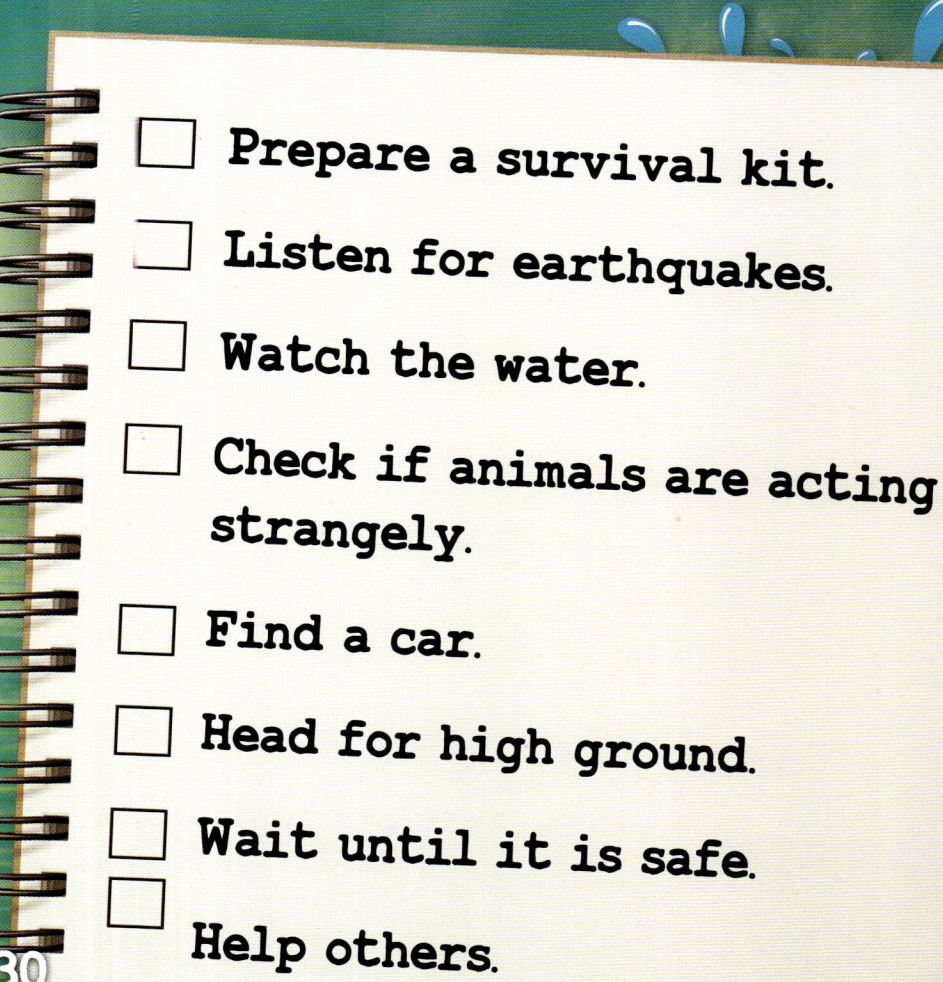

- ☐ Prepare a survival kit.
- ☐ Listen for earthquakes.
- ☐ Watch the water.
- ☐ Check if animals are acting strangely.
- ☐ Find a car.
- ☐ Head for high ground.
- ☐ Wait until it is safe.
- ☐ Help others.

GLOSSARY

AFTERSHOCKS — smaller earthquakes that occur after a larger one

DETECT — to discover or notice something

LANDSLIDE — a large amount of earth and rock that falls down hillsides or mountains, often caused by heavy rain or earthquakes

METEORITE — pieces of rock that enter a planet's atmosphere without being destroyed

RATION — to limit and share out something into set amounts

INDEX

animals 15, 30

bottled water 19, 28

buildings 8, 22, 25

cars 21, 30

coasts 21

food 18, 26

plates 7, 10

radios 13, 16, 24

roads 22

scientists 13

shelters 27

survival kits 16, 20, 26, 30